Slimming World's
fakeaways

takeout...
with the Syns taken out!

We're a nation of takeaway-lovers! Whether it's a Friday night Chinese or a big juicy burger, we love them all – the only problem is that the standard versions can be packed with Syns. Now, with this brilliant book in your kitchen, you can enjoy all the flavour of a takeaway whenever you want… and never have to dial in dinner again!

We've studied the menus of the nation's best-loved takeaways and created fantastic Food Optimised versions of all your favourites. So whether you have a craving for korma, a fondness for fish & chips or a passion for pizza, you'll find something to tempt you.

Every one of our 'fakeaways' is just as delicious as the real thing, plus they're healthier, more filling and with just a fraction of the Syns (in fact, lots are completely Free!). Another bonus is that making your own takeout costs so much less, and you'll soon see a difference in your wallet as well as your waistline.

So throw away that pile of menus today – we've got your perfect takeaway wrapped up!

contents

OPEN 24 HRS A DAY, 7 DAYS A WEEK

Pizza the action

CREATE YOUR OWN SW PIZZA IN 3 EASY STEPS

PERFECT PIZZA EVERY TIME!

SW Fried Chicken

Mains

SW Spiced Chicken
Flavour-packed chicken thighs coated in sensational spiced breadcrumbs p62

BBQ Chicken Drumsticks
Delicious chicken on the bone in a more-ish barbecue sauce p64

Chicken Nuggets
Lip-licking chicken bites to satisfy the biggest appetite p66

Piri Piri Chicken Salad
Tender chicken breast and fresh vegetables with a hot chilli kick ... p69

Sides

Crunchy Coleslaw (v)
The essential side dish for a chicken feast p70

FREE HOME DELIVERY

Curried Away
The authentic taste of India

p74 **LAMB DHANSAK** /
Tender meat and filling lentils

p76 **LAMB ROGAN JOSH** //
Rich, spicy and satisfying

p78 **LAMB VINDALOO** ////
Hot but surprisingly subtle

p81 **CREAMY CHICKEN KORMA** /
Mild and slightly sweet

p82 **TANDOORI CHICKEN** /
Drumsticks roasted in a tasty marinade

p85 **CHICKEN TIKKA MASALA** //
Britain's favourite curry!

p86 **KING PRAWN DOPIAZA** //
Fresh seafood and an aromatic oniony sauce

p88 **VEGETABLE BIRYANI** (v) //
Classic rice dish packed with healthy veg

p90 **SAAG ALOO** (v) /
Potatoes and spinach in mouth-watering spices

p93 **PILAU RICE** (v)
The essential side dish for your curry

English menu available
We do not accept cheques

---

eastern eats

10% discount for collection

Meat Dishes

Szechuan beef /// p96
Pork in black bean sauce / p98
Pork pad thai / p101

Chicken Dishes

Sweet & sour chicken / p102
Thai green chicken curry // p105
Chicken chow mein / p106

Fish Dishes

Thai fish cakes // p108
Special prawn fried rice p110

Vegetarian Dishes

Speedy vegetable noodles with tofu (v) / p112
Thai yellow vegetable curry (v) // .. p115

Sides

Egg fried rice (v) p116

Buffet nights Friday & Saturday

burger nights
and
kebab delights

Create your own American diner with our selection of satisfying burgers and hot dogs. If you prefer a little Middle Eastern magic, we've included a few classic kebabs, too!

cajun chicken burgers

serves 4

each serving is:

7 Syns on Extra Easy

7 Syns on Original

15 Syns on Green

ready in 30 minutes

---

4 skinless and boneless chicken breasts

1 tbsp Cajun seasoning

1 tbsp ground cumin

salt and freshly ground black pepper

low calorie cooking spray

4 tbsp extra-light mayonnaise

2 tbsp fat free fromage frais

4 x 60g wholemeal rolls, halved

1 tomato, thinly sliced

½ red onion, thinly sliced

small handful of baby leaf spinach

for the Cajun ketchup

150g passata

6 tbsp tomato purée

a pinch of sweetener

1 tsp red wine vinegar

1 tsp Cajun seasoning

dash of Worcestershire sauce

Cajun spices come from the southern states of the US and they take chicken to another level – our Cajun ketchup is the perfect accompaniment!

Put all the Cajun ketchup ingredients in a small saucepan and bring to the boil. Reduce the heat to low and cook gently for 8-10 minutes or until thickened. Remove from the heat and leave to cool.

Meanwhile, put the chicken breasts between two sheets of cling film and flatten slightly with a mallet or rolling pin.

Mix the Cajun seasoning and cumin with a good grind of black pepper and a sprinkling of salt. Sprinkle the mixture over the chicken to coat well and lightly spray with low calorie cooking spray.

Place a griddle pan over a high heat. When it's hot, add the chicken and griddle for 5 minutes on each side or until cooked through.

Mix together the mayonnaise and fromage frais and spread over the roll bases. Fill the rolls with tomato, red onion and spinach, then slice the chicken thickly and arrange on top. Spoon over the Cajun ketchup, press the roll lid on top and serve hot with Slimming World chips (page 41) and plenty of salad.

*Save 6 Syns per serving by leaving out the roll, or having it as a **Healthy Extra b** choice.*

ocean burgers

serves 4

each serving is:

7 Syns on Extra Easy

7 Syns on Original

13½ Syns on Green

❄ (uncooked burgers only)

ready in 30 minutes, plus
cooling and chilling

These scrumptious fish and prawn patties are infused with the fresh flavours of spring onions, lemon and parsley – it's a delicious dinner from the deep!

1 slice of wholemeal bread
from a small 400g loaf

400g skinless and boneless
cod or haddock fillets,
roughly chopped

300g peeled raw king
or tiger prawns

bunch of spring onions

finely grated zest of
1 unwaxed lemon

1 tsp garlic salt

small handful of roughly
chopped fresh parsley

a pinch of dried red chilli
flakes (optional)

4 x 60g wholemeal rolls,
halved

a few lettuce leaves

1 tomato, thinly sliced

¼ cucumber, thinly sliced

for the ketchup

150g passata with
onion and garlic

6 tbsp tomato purée

a pinch of sweetener

small handful of finely
chopped fresh basil

Put all the ingredients for the ketchup in a small saucepan and bring to the boil. Reduce the heat to low and cook for 12-15 minutes or until thickened. Remove from the heat and set aside to cool. (This can be made the day before, chilled and brought to room temperature before serving.)

Line a baking tray with non-stick baking parchment.

Place the slice of bread in a food processor and blend until coarsely crumbed. Add the fish and prawns to the breadcrumbs along with the spring onions, lemon zest, garlic salt, parsley and chilli, if using. Pulse briefly, taking care not to over process the mixture.

Tip the mixture into a bowl and divide it into four equal portions using your hands. Shape into burgers and arrange on the prepared baking tray. Chill in the fridge for 30 minutes or overnight if time permits.

Preheat the oven to 220°C/Fan 200°C/Gas 7.

Bake the burgers for about 12-15 minutes or until firm.

Spoon some ketchup into each roll and add the lettuce leaves, tomato, cucumber and burgers. Top with the roll lids and serve hot with extra ketchup on the side. This is delicious with Slimming World chips (page 41) and salad.

*Save 6 Syns per serving by leaving out the roll or having it as a **Healthy Extra b** choice.*

double
bacon burgers

serves 4

each serving is:

6½ Syns on Extra Easy

6½ Syns on Original

18 Syns on Green

❄ (uncooked burgers only)

ready in 30 minutes,
plus chilling

---

1 small onion, finely chopped

500g extra-lean beef mince

small handful of finely
chopped fresh parsley

salt and freshly ground
black pepper

8 lean bacon rashers,
visible fat removed

1 level tbsp extra-light
mayonnaise

2 tbsp fat free natural
fromage frais

4 x 60g wholemeal rolls,
halved (and toasted,
if you like)

a few lettuce leaves

¼ cucumber, thinly sliced

1 tomato, thinly sliced

1 onion, sliced into thin rings

Dive into delicious beef and bacon, plenty of fresh crispy salad and an indulgent layer of creamy mayo, all sandwiched in a wholemeal roll. It's a premium burger to savour!

Place the onion, beef and parsley in a large bowl. Season and mix well with your hands until combined. Divide the mixture into eight equal portions and form each portion into a burger. Place the burgers on a plate lined with baking parchment, cover and chill for 30 minutes.

When you're ready to cook, preheat the grill to high.

Heat a large non-stick frying pan over a high heat then gently press the burgers into the pan – you may need to cook them in two batches. Cook for 1 minute then turn and cook for a further minute to seal. Reduce the heat to medium and cook for a further 5 minutes, turning frequently until cooked through.

Meanwhile, grill the bacon for 3-4 minutes each side or until cooked to your liking.

Remove the burgers and the bacon from the heat and drain on kitchen paper.

Mix the mayonnaise and fromage frais together and spread on both halves of the rolls. Fill with the lettuce, cucumber, tomato, onion, burgers and bacon.

Serve hot with fries (page 41) and plenty of salad.

*Save 6 Syns per serving by leaving out the roll, or having it as a **Healthy Extra b** choice.*

burger
in a bowl

Who says you need bread to enjoy the burger experience? This clever recipe has everything but the roll: juicy beef mince, a stunningly tasty sauce and plenty of fresh salad vegetables too.

serves 4

each serving is:

1 Syn on Extra Easy

1 Syn on Original

9 Syns on Green

ready in 20 minutes

Spray a large, heavy-based non-stick frying pan with low calorie cooking spray and place over a high heat. Add the beef, onion and garlic and stir-fry for 6-7 minutes or until the beef is cooked through and the onions have softened. Season well.

Meanwhile, put all the SW super sauce ingredients in a bowl with 4 tablespoons of water and whisk until well combined.

Mix together the lettuce, gherkins, onions and tomatoes and divide between four wide bowls. Spoon the beef mixture on top, drizzle over the SW super sauce and serve hot.

low calorie cooking spray

500g extra-lean beef mince

1 onion, finely chopped

2 garlic cloves, crushed

salt and freshly ground black pepper

½ iceberg lettuce, roughly shredded

8 gherkins, sliced

1 small red onion, finely chopped

2 tomatoes, roughly chopped

for the SW super sauce

3 level tbsp extra-light mayonnaise

5 tbsp fat free fromage frais

1 level tbsp American-style mustard

2 tbsp tomato purée

2 tsp white wine vinegar

½ tsp garlic salt

¼ tsp onion granules

¼ tsp sweet smoked paprika

spicy mexican
bean burgers

serves 4

each serving is:

1½ **Syns** on Extra Easy

1½ **Syns** on Green

7½ **Syns** on Original

❄ (uncooked burgers only)

ready in about 30 minutes,
plus chilling

2 slices of wholemeal bread
from a small 400g loaf

2 x 400g cans kidney beans,
drained and rinsed

2 tsp smoked paprika

1 tsp ground cumin

large handful of finely
chopped fresh coriander
leaves

finely grated zest of
1 unwaxed lime

1 egg, lightly beaten

salt and freshly ground
black pepper

Beans are super-filling and make a great choice for a meat-free burger. We've given ours a Mexican twist, using smoky spices and zesty lime.

Put the bread into a food processor and blitz to make breadcumbs. Add the beans, paprika, cumin, coriander, lime zest and egg, then season and blitz again until you have a rough paste.

Transfer the mixture into a bowl and divide into eight portions. Using wet hands, shape each portion into a burger and space them apart on a baking sheet. Chill for 6 hours or overnight if time permits.

When you're ready to cook, preheat the oven to 180°C/Fan 160°C/Gas 4.

Bake the burgers for 15-20 minutes, turning halfway, until golden and crisp.

Divide the burgers between plates and serve with plenty of salad.

If you like a bit of heat in your burger, add 2 teaspoons of hot chilli powder with the other spices.

hot dogs

Bring the classic American street food to your table…
with a few twists to make them tastier and healthier.
You'll save around 14 Syns on Extra Easy and Original!

serves 4

each serving is:

6½ Syns on Extra Easy

6½ Syns on Original

10 Syns on Green

ready in 25 minutes

Preheat the grill to medium.

Spray a non-stick frying pan with low calorie cooking spray, add the onions and cook over a low heat for 5 minutes. Add the stock and cook for a further 10 minutes or until tender. Drain off any liquid in the pan.

Meanwhile, grill the sausages for 15-20 minutes, turning halfway.

Put the lettuce leaves, sausages and onions into each roll and serve hot with fries (page 41), ketchup (page 42) and American-style mustard (½ Syn per level teaspoon).

*Have the roll as your **Healthy Extra b** choice and you'll save 6 Syns. You can also make Free mustard by mixing 1 teaspoon of mustard powder with 2 teaspoons of water.*

low calorie cooking spray

2 onions, finely sliced

100ml boiling
vegetable stock

4 Sainsbury's Be Good
to Yourself Extra Lean
Cumberland Pork Sausages*

4 lettuce leaves

4 x 60g wholemeal finger
rolls, sliced open

*These sausages are
½ Syn each on Extra Easy
and Original, and 4 Syns on
Green but Syn values for
branded foods can change.
You can find the very
latest information online at
www.slimmingworld.com/
lifelineonline.*

doner kebabs

serves 4

each serving is:

Free on Extra Easy

Free on Original

8 Syns on Green

ready in about 2 hours, plus chilling and resting

---

low calorie cooking spray

1 onion, finely chopped

3 garlic cloves, crushed

500g extra-lean beef mince

½ tsp ground ginger

1 tsp ground cumin

¼ tsp cinnamon

1 tsp paprika

1 egg, lightly beaten

1 tbsp dried mixed herbs or dried parsley

salt and freshly ground black pepper

a few iceberg lettuce leaves, shredded

½ red onion, sliced

4 tomatoes, sliced

4 large bottled gherkins in vinegar, drained and sliced

lemon wedges, to serve

Turkey's most famous culinary export is traditionally eaten at the end of a night out but our Syn-free version is a treat at any time of day. And you can enjoy it knowing you're saving around 34½ Syns on Extra Easy and Original!

Spray a large, heavy-based non-stick saucepan with low calorie cooking spray and place over a low heat. Add the onion and cook for 12-15 minutes, stirring occasionally, until softened and lightly browned.

Transfer the onion to a food processor and add the garlic, beef, ginger, cumin, cinnamon, paprika, egg and dried mixed herbs. Season well and blend until fairly smooth. Turn out into a bowl.

Spoon the mixture into a non-stick loaf tin (it should fill to a little over halfway up the tin) and pat down. Cover and chill for 4 hours or overnight if time permits.

When you're ready to cook, preheat the oven to 180°C/Fan 160°C/Gas 4.

Cover the loaf tin with foil and bake for 1 hour 20 minutes. Remove from the oven and drain off any liquid, then return to the oven, uncovered, for 10-12 minutes. Leave the tin to rest for 12-15 minutes, then remove the doner meat and slice thinly.

Divide the lettuce, red onion, tomatoes and gherkins between plates. Top with the sliced doner meat and serve with lemon wedges to squeeze over.

Add 1 level tablespoon of chilli sauce to your kebab for just ½ Syn.

Free on Extra Easy and Original

minted
lamb kebabs

Garlic, mint and mustard are magical with lamb and the cherry tomatoes add a burst of squishy goodness.

serves 4

each serving is:

Free on Extra Easy

Free on Original

9½ Syns on Green

ready in 30 minutes,
plus marinating

100g fat free natural yogurt

finely grated zest and juice
of 1 unwaxed lemon

2 garlic cloves, crushed

1 tsp English mustard
powder

2 tbsp tomato purée

500g lean lamb leg steaks,
visible fat removed, cut into
bite-sized pieces

32 yellow and red
cherry tomatoes

small handful of roughly
chopped fresh mint,
to garnish

In a large shallow bowl, mix together the yogurt, lemon zest and juice, garlic, mustard powder and tomato purée. Add the lamb and stir to coat well. Cover and marinate in the fridge for 1 hour or longer if time permits.

Preheat the grill to medium.

Thread the lamb and cherry tomatoes on to eight metal skewers (or wooden skewers that have been soaked in water for 20 minutes), brush with the marinade and grill for 5 minutes on each side or until cooked to your liking.

Transfer the kebabs to warmed plates, sprinkle over the mint and serve hot with a crisp salad.

zesty turkey kebabs
with garlic dip

Turkey is seriously lean and filling and it goes brilliantly with chunks of colourful vegetables on these spicy skewers.

serves 4

each serving is:

Free on Extra Easy

Free on Original

9 Syns on Green

ready in 30 minutes

Preheat the grill to hot.

In a bowl, mix the turkey with the carrot, lemon zest, curry powder and some seasoning. Divide the mixture into 16 pieces and roll each piece into a ball.

Assemble the kebabs by threading the turkey balls, red onion, red pepper, courgette and cherry tomatoes on to eight metal skewers (or wooden skewers soaked in water for 20 minutes). Grill for 8-10 minutes on each side or until cooked through.

Meanwhile, make the dip. Mix the lemon juice, yogurt and garlic together, season to taste and sprinkle with paprika.

These kebabs are best served hot and are delicious with the garlic dip and salad.

500g extra-lean turkey mince

1 carrot, peeled and coarsely grated

zest and juice of 1 unwaxed lemon

1 tbsp medium curry powder

salt and freshly ground black pepper

1 red onion, cut into wedges

1 red pepper, deseeded and cut into bite-sized chunks

1 courgette, cut into bite-sized chunks

16 cherry tomatoes

100g fat free natural yogurt

1 garlic clove, crushed

a pinch of paprika, to serve

spiced vegetable kebabs

Sumac is a zesty, tangy spice that's extremely popular in the Middle East. It's sensational in these satisfying vegetable kebabs.

serves 4

each serving is:

Free on Extra Easy

Free on Green

Free on Original

ready in 35 minutes,
plus marinating

1 tbsp sumac

¼ tsp cinnamon

1 tsp ground cumin

3 garlic cloves, finely grated

3cm piece of root ginger, peeled and finely grated

1 tsp sweet smoked paprika

juice of 2 lemons

salt and freshly ground black pepper

1 courgette, cut into bite-sized pieces

2 red peppers, halved, deseeded and cut into bite-sized pieces

2 yellow peppers, halved, deseeded and cut into bite-sized pieces

1 aubergine, cut into bite-sized pieces

In a large bowl, mix together the sumac, cinnamon, cumin, garlic, ginger, paprika and lemon juice. Season well with salt and pepper and add all the vegetables. Toss to coat evenly, then cover and marinate in the fridge for 20 minutes or overnight if time permits.

When you're ready to cook, preheat the grill to medium-hot.

Thread the vegetable pieces on to eight metal skewers (or wooden skewers soaked in water for 20 minutes) and grill for 6-8 minutes on each side or until lightly charred and cooked through.

These kebabs are best served hot and go really well with couscous and salad.

Sumac is available in larger supermarkets but if you can't get hold of any, use the grated zest of ½ unwaxed lemon instead.

chip shop classics

You'll fall hook, line and sinker for our round-up of traditional treats, including fish & chips, pies and scampi.

BATTERED FISH

FISH CAKES

SCAMPI

STEAK & KIDNEY PIE

CHICKEN PIE

CHIPS

FRENCH FRIES

WEDGES

TARTARE SAUCE

CURRY SAUCE

GRAVY

Free on Extra Easy and Original

battered fish

serves 4

each serving is:

Free on Extra Easy

Free on Original

7 Syns on Green

ready in 25 minutes

---

4 thick skinless cod or haddock fillets

salt and freshly ground black pepper

2 eggs, separated

lemon wedges, to serve

Who can resist those soft flakes of fresh cod or haddock in tempting batter? Our healthy home-cooked version of the classic British takeaway is 100% tasty and it's Free on Extra Easy and Original!

Preheat the oven to 200°C/Fan 180°C/Gas 6.

Line a baking tray with non-stick baking parchment. Arrange the fish on the tray and season well.

Whisk the egg whites in a large bowl until they form soft peaks. Whisk the yolks in another bowl and fold into the egg whites along with a pinch of salt. Stir to mix well and spoon the mixture over the fish.

Bake for 10-12 minutes or until the egg is lightly browned and the fish is cooked through.

Serve with chips (page 41), tartare sauce (page 42), mushy peas and lemon wedges to squeeze over.

Both canned and frozen mushy peas are Free so there's no need to make them from scratch.

fish
cakes

serves 4

each serving is:

1½ **Syns** on Extra Easy

5½ **Syns** on Green

5½ **Syns** on Original

❄ (uncooked fish cakes only)

ready in about 50 minutes, plus chilling

400g potatoes, peeled and chopped

salt and freshly ground black pepper

low calorie cooking spray

1 courgette, coarsely grated

1 carrot, peeled and coarsely grated

400g skinless cod or haddock fillet

small handful of fresh chives

small handful of fresh dill

half a bunch of spring onions, trimmed

60g wholemeal roll, torn into pieces

2 eggs

Fish cakes are a staple of every chip shop menu. Our golden, crisp-crumbed patties are packed with filling fish and vegetables – kids will love them!

Boil the potatoes in a pan of lightly salted boiling water for 12-15 minutes until tender. Drain, mash, season to taste and set aside in a large mixing bowl.

Meanwhile, spray a frying pan with low calorie cooking spray and place over a high heat. Stir-fry the courgette and carrot for 5 minutes then transfer to a sieve and squeeze out any excess liquid with the back of a spoon. Add to the mashed potatoes.

Put the cod, herbs and spring onions into a food processor and blitz briefly (being careful not to blend too smoothly). Add to the mashed potatoes, mix to combine, then divide the mixture into eight portions and shape each one into a fish cake. Cool, cover and chill for 2 hours or overnight if time permits.

When you're ready to cook, preheat the oven to 180°C/Fan 160°C/Gas 4.

Put the roll into a food processor and blitz until you have fine breadcrumbs, then tip them into a wide bowl. Crack the eggs into another wide bowl and beat lightly.

Dip each fish cake in the beaten egg then roll in the breadcrumbs to coat evenly. Arrange the fish cakes on a large non-stick baking tray, spray with low calorie cooking spray and bake for 15-20 minutes or until cooked and golden.

These fish cakes are tastiest served hot with tartare sauce (page 42) and plenty of salad.

king prawn
scampi

serves 4

each serving is:

1 Syn on Extra Easy

1 Syn on Original

3 Syns on Green

ready in 30 minutes

Scampi is traditionally made with langoustines (Dublin Bay prawns) – ours are made with king prawns, which are easier to buy and just as much of a treat.

40g wholemeal bread

2 tsp dried mixed herbs

1 tbsp paprika

2 eggs

salt and freshly ground black pepper

24 peeled raw king prawns, tails left on if you like

low calorie cooking spray

Preheat the oven to 220°C/Fan 200°C/Gas 7.

Put the bread in a food processor and blitz until you have fine breadcrumbs. Transfer to a shallow bowl and mix in the dried herbs and paprika.

Lightly beat the eggs in another shallow bowl.

Season the prawns, then dip each one first into the egg and then the breadcrumb mixture. Arrange the prawns on a non-stick baking sheet, lightly spray with low calorie cooking spray and bake for 10-12 minutes or until cooked through and lightly browned.

These are delicious served hot with chips (page 41), tartare sauce (page 42) and a big mixed salad or mushy peas.

steak and kidney pies

A good pie is fantastic comfort food on a cold night –
and making yours at home saves you up to 20 Syns and
a chilly walk to the chip shop!

serves 4

each serving is:

4½ **Syns** on Extra Easy

4½ **Syns** on Original

10½ **Syns** on Green

ready in 45 minutes

Spray a large pan with low calorie cooking spray and place over a high heat.
Add the steak, kidneys, carrot, celery, mushrooms, onion, Worcestershire
sauce, garlic salt, thyme, beef stock and gravy granules. Bring to the boil and
cook over a high heat, stirring occasionally, for 6-8 minutes or until thickened.
Divide the mixture between four individual pie dishes.

Preheat your oven to 220°C/Fan 200°C/Gas 7.

Roll out the pastry on baking parchment and cut out four lids, big enough
to cover the pie dishes. Brush the rim of each dish with a little egg, add the
pastry lids and seal the edges with a fork. Make a hole in the top of each pie,
then brush the lid with more egg. Bake for 15-20 minutes or until the pastry
has risen.

This pie is delicious with Slimming World chips (page 41) and salad or
mushy peas.

low calorie cooking spray

300g beef frying steak,
visible fat removed, cut
into bite-sized pieces

100g lambs' kidneys,
white cores removed,
roughly chopped

1 carrot, peeled
and finely diced

1 celery stick, finely diced

200g baby button
mushrooms, halved
or quartered if large

1 onion, finely chopped

2 tbsp Worcestershire sauce

1 tsp garlic salt

1 tsp finely chopped
fresh thyme

300ml boiling beef stock

1 level tsp gravy granules

100g ready-rolled light
puff pastry

1 egg, lightly beaten

chicken, ham and mushroom pies

serves 4

each serving is:

3 Syns on Extra Easy

3 Syns on Original

16½ Syns on Green

ready in 1 hour

500ml boiling chicken stock

4 skinless and boneless chicken breasts, cut into bite-sized pieces

2 onions, roughly chopped

1 garlic clove, finely chopped

2 carrots, peeled and diced

200g green beans, chopped

200g button mushrooms, halved or quartered if large

1 level tsp chicken gravy granules

2 tbsp tomato purée

2 x 200g cans cooked lean ham, diced

small handful of finely chopped fresh tarragon

salt and freshly ground black pepper

1 egg, lightly beaten

70g ready-rolled light puff pastry

Chicken and ham are perfect partners in a pie, and the pretty lattice pastry tops make our versions much lower in Syns.

Put the stock, chicken, onions, garlic, carrots, beans and mushrooms in a pan over a medium heat and cook for 15-20 minutes, stirring often, until the onions have softened and the chicken is cooked.

Add the gravy granules and tomato purée and stir well. Add the ham and tarragon, season and stir again.

Preheat the oven to 180°C/Fan 160°C/Gas 4.

Transfer the chicken mixture to four individual pie dishes. Brush the rims of the dishes with some of the beaten egg.

Roll out the pastry, cut it into strips and arrange over the pies in a lattice pattern. Brush the pastry with the remaining egg and bake for 15-20 minutes or until the pastry is puffed up and golden. Serve with Slimming World chips (page 41) or salad.

chips with everything!

Whatever you're planning to tuck into on your fakeaway night,
you know it'll be even better with a side order of chips, fries or wedges!

slimming world chips

serves 4

each serving is:

Free on Extra Easy

Free on Green

9½ **Syns** on Original

ready in 40 minutes

1kg floury potatoes,
such as King Edward or
Maris Piper, peeled and
thickly cut into chips

low calorie cooking spray

salt

Preheat the oven to 200°C/
Fan 180°C/Gas 6. Boil the chips
in lightly salted boiling water for
5 minutes. Drain well, return
to the pan and cover. Leave
to cool slightly then shake the
pan to roughen the edges.
Line a baking tray with baking
parchment and arrange the
chips in a single layer. Spray
with low calorie cooking spray
and bake for 20 minutes or
until golden. Season with salt
to serve. You'll find recipes for
ketchup, curry sauce and gravy
on page 42.

french fries

serves 4

each serving is:

Free on Extra Easy

Free on Green

9½ **Syns** on Original

ready in 30 minutes

1kg floury potatoes,
such as King Edward or
Maris Piper, peeled and
thinly cut into fries

low calorie cooking spray

salt

Preheat the oven to 200°C/
Fan 180°C/Gas 6. Boil the fries
in lightly salted boiling water
for 1-2 minutes, then drain and
spread out on a baking tray lined
with baking parchment. Spray
with low calorie cooking spray
and bake for 12-15 minutes or
until lightly golden. Season with
salt to serve.

spiced sweet potato wedges

serves 4

each serving is:

Free on Extra Easy

Free on Green

11 **Syns** on Original

ready in 40 minutes

---

4 sweet potatoes, peeled
and cut into wedges

1 tsp smoked paprika

2 tsp cumin seeds

1 tsp ground cinnamon

low calorie cooking spray

salt

Preheat the oven to 200°C/
Fan 180°C/Gas 6. Mix the spices
in a shallow bowl. Spray the
wedges with low calorie cooking
spray and toss in the spices until
they're evenly coated. Arrange
the wedges in a single layer on
a baking tray lined with baking
parchment and bake for 30-35
minutes or until tender. Season
with salt to serve.

skinny dips

ketchup

serves 4 ❄

each serving is:

Free on all choices

ready in 1 hour

Free on all choices

Put 1 finely chopped onion, 2 crushed garlic cloves, 2 x 400g cans chopped tomatoes, 2 teaspoons of ground cinnamon, 2 teaspoons of celery salt, 2 teaspoons of mustard powder, 2 teaspoons of ground white pepper, 2 tablespoons of sweetener, 250ml red wine vinegar and 1 tablespoon of Worcestershire sauce into a saucepan over a high heat and bring to the boil. Reduce the heat to low and cook gently for 45 minutes, stirring occasionally. Remove the pan from the heat, season with salt and leave to cool. Blitz with a stick blender or in a food processor and sieve the ketchup into a bowl. Leftover ketchup can be kept in a sterilised airtight jar in the fridge for up to 3 weeks.

gravy

serves 4 ❄ Ⓥ

each serving is:

1 Syn on all choices

ready in 25 minutes

Spray a pan with low calorie cooking spray and place over a medium heat. Add 2 red onions (cut into wedges) and 1 crushed garlic clove and cook until soft. Add 425ml boiling vegetable stock and continue to cook for a further 10 minutes. Mix 1 level tablespoon of cornflour with 1 tablespoon of water to make a paste. Add to the gravy, reduce the heat and simmer, stirring continuously, until thickened. Blitz with a stick blender or in a food processor and serve hot with chips. Leftover gravy can be kept in the fridge, covered, for up to 4 days.

curry sauce

serves 4 Ⓥ

each serving is:

Free on all choices

ready in 30 minutes

Free on all choices

Spray a pan with low calorie cooking spray and place over a medium heat. Add 1 roughly chopped onion and 2 crushed garlic cloves and cook until soft. Add a 1cm piece of root ginger, peeled and finely grated, and cook for 1-2 minutes, then add 1 tablespoon of curry powder and cook for a further 1-2 minutes. Add a 400g can chopped tomatoes, 60ml boiling vegetable stock and 2 tablespoons of sweetener and bring to the boil. Reduce the heat and simmer for 12-15 minutes. Blitz with a stick blender, add 50g fat free natural fromage frais and a small handful of chopped fresh coriander and mint and gently heat through (be careful not to let it boil). Serve hot with chips. Leftover curry sauce can be kept in the fridge, covered, for up to 3 days.

tartare sauce

serves 4 Ⓥ

each serving is:

½ Syn on all choices

ready in 10 minutes

In a bowl, mix together 4 tablespoons of drained and roughly chopped bottled gherkins, 1 finely chopped small red onion, 1 tablespoon of drained and rinsed capers, 2 tablespoons of extra-light mayonnaise, 200g fat free fromage frais and 1 tablespoon of finely grated unwaxed lemon zest. Season, scatter over a little chopped fresh dill and chill until ready to serve. Leftover tartare sauce can be kept in the fridge, covered, for up to 3 days.

Pizza the action

Takeaway pizzas are one of the nation's favourite treats but they're so high in Syns – a takeout meat feast, for example, comes in at 13 Syns per 100g slice. Although we can't make pizza Free, these home-made versions will be life-savers on those occasions when nothing else will do! Just follow our three easy steps and you'll be serving up perfect pizza every time.

step 1   Make our basic dough and roll it into your chosen shape (page 46).

step 2   Pick a sauce to spread over the base – tomato, bianca or houmous (page 48).

step 3   Choose a tempting topping from our selection (pages 50-58) – or invent your own!

step 1
make the dough

pizza dough

makes 1 pizza,
big enough to serve 4

each serving (base only) is:

5½ **Syns** on Extra Easy

5½ **Syns** on Green

5½ **Syns** on Original

ready in 20 minutes

125g strong bread flour

7g sachet instant active yeast

1 tsp salt

Put the flour into a large bowl and stir in the yeast and salt. Make a well in the middle, pour in 75ml of warm water and mix with a wooden spoon until you have soft, fairly wet dough. Dust a surface very lightly with flour (1 level teaspoon is 1 Syn), turn out the dough and knead for 5 minutes until smooth. Cover with a tea towel until you're ready to roll. (You don't need to let the dough rise if you're making a thin crust.)

On a very lightly floured surface, use a rolling pin to roll out the dough into a very thin circle about 22cm across (or roll any other shape you like – see 'Ready to roll', below).

Slide your pizza base onto a preheated pizza stone or baking sheet (line the baking sheet with baking parchment just before you add the pizza base). You're now ready to add your pizza sauce (choose from tomato, bianca and houmous on page 48) and your preferred topping (see our selection on pages 50-58 or invent your own).

dough balls and a quick garlic dip

Using the same basic dough recipe, you can make a batch of dough balls for just 1 Syn each! Preheat the oven to 200°C/Fan 180°/Gas 6. Using your hands, shape the dough into 24 dough balls and space them well apart on a baking sheet sprayed with low calorie cooking spray. Sprinkle over 1 crushed garlic clove, some finely chopped rosemary, paprika and salt and bake for 10-12 minutes.

To make a delicious Free garlic dip for your dough balls, just mix 200g quark, 200g fat free fromage frais, 1 crushed garlic clove, 2 finely chopped spring onions and 1 tablespoon of cider vinegar. Season with salt and freshly ground black pepper and chill until you're ready to serve.

ready to roll

Pizzas don't have to be round. If you're feeling creative you could roll out a square, rectangle or four mini pizzas (reduce the baking time by 5 minutes). For a lighter ring-shaped pizza (3½ Syns per serving, based on four servings), make up the dough as above but reduce the flour to 75g and water to 45ml. Push your fingers through the middle to make a ring then gradually make the hole bigger and bigger.

dough without

You don't have to use dough to enjoy a great pizza. For a pizza base that's Free on Extra Easy and Original, use a flattened skinless chicken breast or turkey breast steak. For a vegetarian version, use giant portobello mushrooms.

step *pick a sauce*

2

make it saucy!

tomato
pizza sauce

makes enough for 1 pizza,
big enough to serve 4

Free on all choices

❄️ Ⓥ

ready in 35 minutes

4 shallots, finely chopped

3 garlic cloves, crushed

2 tsp dried oregano

400g can chopped tomatoes

4 tbsp tomato purée

small handful of finely
chopped fresh basil

salt and freshly ground
black pepper

Put the shallots, garlic, oregano,
chopped tomatoes, tomato
purée and most of the basil
into a saucepan. Cook over
a medium-low heat for 25
minutes, until you have a thick,
spreadable sauce. Season
well, scatter over a little more
chopped basil and spread over
your pizza base. Now you're
ready to add your topping
(see pages 50-58).

Say cheese: *For a classic
margherita pizza, spread this
sauce over your pizza base
and add 65g of sliced light
mozzarella (1½ Syns per serving
if you're feeding four). Bake for
15-20 minutes at 200°C/
Fan 180°C/Gas 6.*

bianca
pizza sauce

makes enough for 1 pizza,
big enough to serve 4

Free on all choices

Ⓥ

ready in 25 minutes

low calorie cooking spray

1 onion, finely chopped

2 garlic cloves, crushed

300g low fat natural
cottage cheese

100g quark

salt and freshly ground
black pepper

1 tsp roughly chopped fresh
oregano (or 1 tsp dried oregano)

Spray a non-stick frying pan with
low calorie cooking spray and
place over a medium heat. Add
the onion and cook for 8 minutes,
then add the garlic and cook for
2 minutes. Put the onion, garlic,
cottage cheese and quark into a
food processor and blitz briefly to
make a rough paste. Season well
and scatter over the oregano.
Spread over your pizza base and
choose one of our five fantastic
toppings (see pages 50-58).

Keep it simple: *This sauce
makes a great topping in its
own right – spread it over your
pizza base and bake for 15-20
minutes at 200°C/Fan 180°C/
Gas 6 for a bianca pizza.*

houmous
pizza sauce

makes more than enough for
1 pizza, big enough to serve 4

Free on Extra Easy and Green,
3 Syns per serving on Original

Ⓥ

ready in 10 minutes

400g can chickpeas, drained

1 garlic clove, crushed

2 tbsp lemon juice,
plus extra to taste

2 tbsp fat free natural
Greek yogurt

salt and freshly ground
black pepper

a pinch of smoked paprika
or cayenne pepper (optional)

Tip the chickpeas into a food
processor along with the garlic,
lemon juice and yogurt. Pulse
until fairly smooth, then season
well, add more lemon juice to
taste and pulse again. Sprinkle
with smoked paprika or cayenne
pepper if you like your houmous
a little spicier! Spread over your
pizza base and choose one of
our five fantastic toppings (see
pages 50-58).

Dip tip: *Houmous is a delicious
alternative to tomato sauce on
pizzas. Try it with our griddled
Mediterranean vegetable
topping (page 50).*

griddled mediterranean vegetable pizza

serves 4

each serving (including the dough) is:

5½ **Syns** on Extra Easy

5½ **Syns** on Green

5½ **Syns** on Original

Ⓥ

ready in 30 minutes, plus 15-20 minutes to bake the pizza

---

low calorie cooking spray

1 red pepper, halved, deseeded and sliced

1 yellow pepper, halved, deseeded and sliced

1 small red onion, cut into thin wedges

3 baby courgettes, thinly sliced or peeled into ribbons with a potato peeler

small handful of fresh basil leaves, to garnish

Mediterranean veg are made to be chargrilled and this super-healthy topping tastes as spectacular as it looks.

Make and roll out your pizza dough (page 46), then spread with pizza sauce (page 48).

Preheat the oven to 200°C/Fan 180°C/Gas 6.

Spray a large griddle pan with low calorie cooking spray and place over a high heat. In batches, cook the peppers, onion and courgettes for about 3-4 minutes on each side or until lightly charred.

Arrange the peppers, onion and courgettes on top of your pizza and bake for 15-20 minutes, until the vegetables are tender and the pizza base is golden.

Scatter over the basil leaves and serve hot.

ham and portobello mushroom ring pizza

Ham and mushroom – or *prosciutto e funghi* if you want to go all Italian – is a classic combination that always satisfies!

Make and roll out your pizza dough (we used a ring-shaped pizza, saving 2 Syns per serving on our basic dough recipe – see 'Ready to roll', page 46). Spread with pizza sauce (page 48).

Preheat the oven to 200°C/Fan 180°C/Gas 6.

Arrange the mushrooms and ham over the top of the pizza, scatter with the oregano and bake for 15-20 minutes, or until the mushrooms are tender and the base is golden.

Fill the middle with rocket leaves and serve hot.

serves 4

each serving (including the dough) is:

3½ Syns on Extra Easy

3½ Syns on Original

5 Syns on Green

ready in 10 minutes, plus 15-20 minutes to bake the pizza

75g portobello mushrooms, sliced, halved or quartered

100g lean ham, visible fat removed, cut into bite-sized pieces

small handful of roughly chopped fresh oregano

large handful of rocket leaves

caramelised onion and goat's cheese pizza

serves 4

each serving (including the dough) is:

7 Syns on Extra Easy

7 Syns on Green

7 Syns on Original

ready in 50 minutes, plus 15-20 minutes to bake the pizza

---

low calorie cooking spray

4 large onions, halved and thinly sliced

2 garlic cloves, finely chopped

1 tbsp balsamic vinegar

1 tsp dried thyme

200g cherry tomatoes, halved or quartered

40g soft goat's cheese, crumbled

salt and freshly ground black pepper

fresh thyme sprigs, to garnish (optional)

Cooking the onions slowly over a low heat makes them super sweet and a perfect match for the creaminess of the goat's cheese.

Make and roll out your pizza dough (page 46). We didn't use a sauce for this pizza but if you want to add one, you'll find them on page 48.

Preheat the oven to 200°C/Fan 180°C/Gas 6.

Spray a wide, heavy-based non-stick frying pan or saucepan with low calorie cooking spray and place over a low heat. Add the onions and cook for 35-40 minutes until lightly golden and very soft. Add the garlic, balsamic vinegar and dried thyme and cook for another 2-3 minutes.

Remove the onion mixture from the heat and spread evenly over your pizza, leaving a narrow border around the edges. Scatter over the cherry tomatoes and the goat's cheese.

Season well and bake for 15-20 minutes or until the base is golden (we made four mini pizzas, which only need 10-15 minutes in the oven). Scatter over the thyme sprigs, if using, and serve hot.

ricotta and
spinach pizza

Italian ricotta cheese is light, creamy and tastes sensational paired with spinach and nutmeg.

Make and roll out your pizza dough (page 46), then spread with pizza sauce (page 48).

Preheat the oven to 200°C/Fan 180°C/Gas 6.

Scatter the spinach leaves over the pizza and grate a little nutmeg over the leaves. Spoon dollops of ricotta on top and sprinkle chilli flakes over the ricotta.

Season well and bake for 15-20 minutes or until the base is golden.

serves 4

each serving (including the dough) is:

7½ **Syns** on Extra Easy

7½ **Syns** on Green

7½ **Syns** on Original

ready in 5 minutes, plus
15-20 minutes to bake the pizza

---

large handful of baby
spinach leaves

a little grated nutmeg

120g ricotta

a pinch of dried red chilli flakes

step **3** choose a topping

meat feast
pizza

serves 4

each serving (including the dough) is:

7 Syns on Extra Easy

7 Syns on Original

14 Syns on Green

ready in 25 minutes, plus 15-20 minutes to bake the pizza

---

low calorie cooking spray

1 onion, finely chopped

2 garlic cloves, finely crushed

250g extra-lean beef mince

tomato pizza sauce (page 48)

6 lean bacon rashers, visible fat removed, cut into small strips

70g light mozzarella, diced

salt and freshly ground black pepper

small handful of fresh basil leaves, to garnish

Meat-lovers will adore this slice of pizza perfection, piled high with beef mince and bacon plus a scattering of melty mozzarella!

Make and roll out your pizza dough (page 46).

Spray a non-stick frying pan with low calorie cooking spray and place over a medium heat. Add the onion, garlic and beef and cook for 5 minutes or until the beef is browned. Stir in the tomato pizza sauce, reduce the heat and cook gently for 8-10 minutes or until the beef is cooked through.

Meanwhile, put the bacon in another non-stick frying pan over a medium heat. Fry for 5 minutes or until cooked through and set aside.

Preheat the oven to 200°C/Fan 180°C/Gas 6.

Spoon the beef over your pizza base and scatter the bacon strips and mozzarella pieces on top. Season and bake for 15-20 minutes or until the base is golden. Scatter over the basil leaves.

This pizza is best served hot and is delicious with a big mixed salad.

fakeaways | **pizza the action**

SW fried chicken

Who needs the Colonel? Our not-so-secret recipes include all your takeaway chicken favourites, packed with flavour and a fraction of the Syns!

SW spiced chicken

serves 4

each serving is:

1½ Syns on Extra Easy

1½ Syns on Original

21 Syns on Green

ready in 45 minutes

Our take on southern fried chicken tastes even better than the high street version thanks to our irresistible spiced breadcrumbs!

150g tomato purée

2 tsp cayenne pepper

2 tsp garlic salt

1 tbsp dried mixed herbs

freshly ground black pepper

1 egg white

60g wholemeal roll, torn into pieces

12 skinless and boneless chicken thighs

low calorie cooking spray

small handful of finely chopped fresh flatleaf parsley, to garnish

lemon wedges, to serve

Preheat your oven to 220°C/Fan 200°C/Gas 7 and line a baking sheet with non-stick baking parchment.

Mix the tomato purée, cayenne pepper, garlic salt and mixed herbs in a large bowl and season with black pepper. Whisk the egg white in a clean glass bowl until stiff peaks form, then fold into the tomato purée mixture.

Whizz the torn roll in a food processor until you have fine crumbs, then transfer to a plate.

Dip the chicken thighs into the egg mixture then roll in the breadcrumbs to coat evenly. Arrange the pieces in a single layer on the prepared baking sheet. Spray with low calorie cooking spray and bake for 25-30 minutes or until cooked through.

Scatter with parsley and serve hot with chips (page 41), coleslaw (page 70) and lemon wedges.

bbq chicken
drumsticks

serves 4

each serving is:

½ **Syn** on Extra Easy

½ **Syn** on Original

11½ **Syns** on Green

ready in 35 minutes,
plus marinating

8 tbsp dark soy sauce

1 level tbsp runny honey

2 tsp garlic salt

2 tsp ground ginger

2 tbsp passata

4 tbsp white wine vinegar

8 chicken drumsticks,
skinned

Enjoy the lip-licking flavours of a good barbecue all year round with these more-ish chicken drumsticks.

In a large bowl, whisk together the soy sauce, honey, garlic salt, ginger, passata and vinegar. Add the drumsticks and toss to coat evenly. Cover and marinate in the fridge for 4 hours or overnight if time permits.

When you're ready to cook, preheat the oven to 200°C/Fan 180°C/Gas 6.

Arrange the drumsticks in a non-stick roasting tin and cook for 20-25 minutes or until cooked through, turning often.

Serve hot with spiced sweet potato wedges (page 41) and corn cobs.

For grilled corn on the cob, preheat the grill to medium-high. Spray your corn cobs with low calorie cooking spray and grill for about 10 minutes, turning occasionally. If you like a bit of spice you could also sprinkle with chilli or your favourite spices before grilling. Season well and scatter with finely chopped fresh parsley. Corn cobs are Free on Extra Easy and Green, and 5 Syns per mini cob on Original.

chicken nuggets

serves 4

each serving is:

1½ **Syns** on Extra Easy

1½ **Syns** on Original

9½ **Syns** on Green

ready in 40 minutes

Succulent chunks of chicken breast coated in herby breadcrumbs make this a fakeaway to remember! You'll save 7½ Syns on a box of six nuggets from the takeaway.

low calorie cooking spray

60g wholemeal roll, torn into pieces

1 tsp mustard powder

2 tsp dried mixed herbs

2 eggs

4 skinless and boneless chicken breasts, sliced thickly

Preheat the oven to 200°C/Fan 180°C/Gas 6, then line a baking sheet with non-stick baking parchment and spray with low calorie cooking spray.

Whizz the torn roll in a food processor until you have fine crumbs, then transfer to a shallow bowl. Add the mustard powder and dried herbs and mix well.

Lightly beat the eggs in another shallow bowl.

Dip the chicken pieces in the egg then roll them in the breadcrumbs to coat each piece evenly. Arrange the pieces on the prepared baking sheet and bake for 20-25 minutes or until cooked through.

Serve hot with French fries (page 41) and baked beans.

piri piri chicken salad

Portuguese piri piri chicken has become one of our favourite takeouts and this substantial salad is definitely one for those who like it hot!

Preheat the oven to 200°C/Fan 180°C/Gas 6.

Put the chicken in a non-stick roasting tin, rub with the garlic and piri piri seasoning and season well. Spray with low calorie cooking spray and roast for 25-30 minutes or until cooked through.

Meanwhile, put all the vegetables in a large bowl, add the vinaigrette, season and toss to mix well.

Thickly slice the chicken and mix into the salad. Scatter over the coriander to serve.

You can buy ready-made piri piri spices or make your own by mixing together 2 teaspoons of paprika, 2 teaspoons of chilli powder (mild, medium or hot), 1 teaspoon of dried oregano, 3 teaspoons of garlic salt and 3 teaspoons of onion granules. For more (or less) heat, adjust the amounts of chilli and paprika.

serves 4

each serving is:

Free on Extra Easy

Free on Original

8 Syns on Green

ready in 35 minutes

4 skinless and boneless chicken breasts

4 garlic cloves, crushed

2 tbsp piri piri seasoning

salt and freshly ground black pepper

low calorie cooking spray

2 Little Gem lettuces, leaves separated

3 tomatoes, halved, deseeded and cut into wedges

½ cucumber, halved and sliced

1 small red onion, halved and thinly sliced

1 yellow pepper, deseeded and thinly sliced

5 tbsp fat free vinaigrette

small handful of chopped fresh coriander, to garnish

crunchy coleslaw

serves 4

each serving is:

Free on Extra Easy

Free on Green

Free on Original

ready in 15 minutes

Crisp, fresh coleslaw is sensational with chicken or burgers, and it's a great way to get plenty of vegetables into your fakeaway!

2 carrots, peeled and coarsely grated

¼ white cabbage, finely shredded

juice of 1 lemon

2 tbsp fat free natural fromage frais

salt and freshly ground black pepper

Put the carrots and cabbage into a large serving bowl.

Add the lemon juice and fromage frais, season to taste with salt and freshly ground black pepper, and stir well to combine.

Chill until you're ready to eat.

curried away

Spice up your life with our sizzling collection of irresistible Indian dishes – all even tastier than a takeaway!

heat guide
/ mild
// medium
/// hot

lamb
dhansak

serves 4

each serving is:

Free on Extra Easy

2½ **Syns** on Original

9½ **Syns** on Green

❄

ready in 1 hour 50 minutes

Filling lentils are at the heart of a good dhansak and ours features chunks of tender lamb and juicy cherry tomatoes too.

low calorie cooking spray

1 onion, finely chopped

1 carrot, peeled and roughly chopped

1 red pepper, deseeded and roughly chopped

1 garlic clove, crushed

2cm piece of root ginger, peeled and finely grated

1 tbsp tandoori spice mix or medium curry powder

500g lean lamb leg steaks, visible fat removed, cut into bite-sized chunks

250g cherry tomatoes

400g can green lentils

300ml boiling lamb stock

salt and freshly ground black pepper

fresh coriander sprigs, to garnish

lime wedges, to serve

Spray a large, deep non-stick frying pan with low calorie cooking spray and place over a medium heat. Cook the onion, carrot and pepper for 10 minutes then add the garlic, ginger and spice mix or curry powder and cook for a further 2 minutes, stirring continuously.

Stir in the lamb, tomatoes, lentils (including the water in the can) and stock. Season well and bring to the boil. Cover, turn the heat down to low and cook for 1 hour 30 minutes or until the lamb is tender.

Check the seasoning, garnish with coriander sprigs and serve hot with lime wedges and boiled basmati rice.

Turn basmati rice into turmeric rice by adding ½ teaspoon of turmeric to the water while the rice is cooking.

lamb
rogan josh

This rich and meaty north Indian stew is infused with enticing spices that leave a lovely warmth in your mouth. We've added carrots and swede, though you could use other root vegetables like potato or parsnip instead.

serves 4

each serving is:

Free on Extra Easy

Free on Original

9½ Syns on Green

❄

ready in 2 hours

---

low calorie cooking spray

500g lean lamb leg steaks, visible fat removed, cut into bite-sized chunks

2 onions, finely chopped

3 garlic cloves, crushed

2cm piece of root ginger, peeled and finely grated

2 cinnamon sticks

2 tsp chilli powder

2 tsp paprika

1 tsp cardamom seeds, crushed

4 tbsp medium curry powder

400g can chopped tomatoes

1 tsp sweetener

600ml boiling lamb stock

2 carrots, peeled and cut into bite-sized pieces

1 swede, peeled and cut into bite-sized pieces

salt and freshly ground black pepper

small handful of finely chopped fresh coriander, to garnish

Spray a large, heavy-based casserole pan with low calorie cooking spray and place over a medium-high heat. Add the lamb and cook for 4 minutes, stirring, or until browned (you may need to do this in batches). Transfer the lamb to a plate with a slotted spoon.

Spray the casserole pan with low calorie cooking spray again and add the onions. Cook over a medium heat for 10 minutes, stirring often, until soft and lightly browned.

Add the garlic, ginger, cinnamon, chilli powder, paprika and cardamom seeds. Stir-fry for 2 minutes then add the curry powder and return the lamb to the pan. Stir-fry for 2-3 minutes then stir in the tomatoes, sweetener, stock, carrots and swede. Season well and bring the mixture to a boil.

Reduce the heat to low and cover tightly. Simmer gently for 1 hour 30 minutes or until the lamb is meltingly tender.

Remove from the heat, scatter over the coriander and serve with rice of your choice.

lamb
vindaloo

Usually the hottest dish on the takeaway menu, this curry isn't for the faint-hearted but the flavourings are subtler than you might think.

serves 4

each serving is:

Free on Extra Easy

Free on Original

9½ **Syns** on Green

❄

ready in 1 hour 40 minutes, plus marinating and resting

125ml white wine vinegar

1 onion, finely chopped

2 tsp ground cumin

2 tsp black mustard seeds, crushed

8 garlic cloves, crushed

2cm piece of root ginger, peeled and finely grated

1 tbsp hot chilli powder

½ tsp ground cloves

1 tsp ground cinnamon

500g lean lamb leg steaks, visible fat removed, cut into bite-sized chunks

400g can chopped tomatoes

¼ tsp sweetener

salt and freshly ground black pepper

small handful of finely chopped fresh coriander, to garnish

lime wedges, to serve

Put the vinegar in a large bowl with the onion, cumin, mustard seeds, garlic, ginger, chilli powder, cloves and cinnamon and a little water. Mix well to form a smooth paste, then add the lamb and stir to coat evenly. Cover the bowl and chill for 4 hours or overnight if you have time.

Put 200ml of water into a large pan over a high heat. Add the lamb mixture, tomatoes and sweetener and bring to the boil. Reduce the heat to low, season well, cover tightly and simmer gently for 1 hour 30 minutes or until the meat is tender.

Remove the pan from the heat and leave to rest for 10 minutes. Scatter over the coriander and serve with boiled basmati rice and lime wedges.

creamy
chicken korma

If you love a good curry but prefer to turn down the heat, korma is for you. This milder Indian dish is gently warming with a delicious sweetness – our version will save you an amazing 16½ Syns on Extra Easy and Original.

serves 4

each serving is:

Free on Extra Easy

Free on Original

8 Syns on Green

❋ (without the fromage frais)

ready in 45 minutes

Spray a large non-stick frying pan with low calorie cooking spray and place over a high heat. Add the bay leaves, cinnamon stick, cardamom seeds, cloves, cumin seeds and onion and stir-fry for 5 minutes.

Add the coriander and ground cumin, curry powder, ginger, garlic and tomatoes and stir-fry for another 3-4 minutes.

Put the chicken into the pan, pour in the stock and bring to the boil. Season well, cover tightly, reduce the heat to low and simmer gently for 20-25 minutes, stirring occasionally.

Remove the pan from the heat and stir in the fromage frais. Scatter over the mint and serve hot with your choice of rice.

low calorie cooking spray

3 bay leaves

1 cinnamon stick

1 tsp cardamom seeds, crushed

¼ tsp ground cloves

2 tsp cumin seeds

1 onion, finely chopped

1 tbsp ground coriander

1 tbsp ground cumin

2 tsp mild curry powder

3cm piece of root ginger, peeled and finely grated

3 garlic cloves, finely crushed

½ x 400g can chopped tomatoes

4 skinless and boneless chicken breasts, cut into bite-sized pieces

200ml boiling chicken stock

salt and freshly ground black pepper

5 tbsp fat free natural fromage frais

small handful of roughly chopped fresh mint, to garnish

tandoori chicken

Tandoori dishes are traditionally prepared in hot clay ovens but your oven at home will cook this curry house classic just as well!

serves 4

each serving is:

Free on Extra Easy

Free on Original

16½ Syns on Green

ready in 35 minutes, plus marinating

12 chicken drumsticks

juice of 1 lemon, plus wedges to serve

½ tsp salt

small handful of finely chopped fresh coriander, to garnish

for the marinade

1 onion, roughly chopped

3 garlic cloves, crushed

2.5cm piece of root ginger, peeled and chopped

½ red chilli, deseeded and roughly chopped

1 tsp ground coriander

1 tsp ground cumin

1 tsp ground black pepper

275g fat free natural yogurt

First skin the chicken drumsticks. Use kitchen paper to help you grip the bony end as you pull the skin over the thicker end. Make two or three deep cuts in each drumstick and put the chicken in a large dish. Sprinkle over the lemon juice and salt and rub into the cuts.

To make the marinade, put the onion, garlic, ginger and chilli in a blender or food processor and blend until smooth. Add the ground spices and yogurt and blend again. Pour the marinade over the drumsticks, stir to coat well then cover and chill for 4 hours or overnight if possible.

When you're ready to cook, preheat the oven to 200°C/Fan 180°C/Gas 6.

Remove the drumsticks from the marinade and space them out in a roasting tin. Roast them for 20-25 minutes until cooked through and slightly charred, turning and brushing with any remaining marinade after 10 minutes.

Scatter the drumsticks with chopped coriander. They are delicious served with rice, salad and lemon wedges.

chicken tikka masala //

It's no wonder that chicken tikka masala has become one of Britain's favourite takeaways. The mouth-watering sauce is truly irresistible – and in our version, tender chunks of marinated chicken breast are grilled on skewers for extra flavour. Best of all, you'll save 14½ Syns on Extra Easy and Original.

In a large dish, mix together the lime juice, yogurt and 3 tablespoons of the tikka curry powder. Season well, then add the chicken and toss to coat well. Marinate in the fridge for 4 hours or overnight if time permits.

When you're ready to cook, preheat the grill to medium.

Spray a large non-stick frying pan with low calorie cooking spray and place over a medium heat. Add the onion, garlic, ginger, chilli, cinnamon, cumin and remaining tikka curry powder and fry for 2-3 minutes. Stir in the tomato purée and 250ml of water. Bring to the boil, reduce the heat to low and simmer for 12-15 minutes, stirring often.

Meanwhile, thread the chicken pieces on to metal skewers, spray with low calorie cooking spray and grill for 12-15 minutes or until cooked through, turning occasionally. Remove the chicken from the skewers and stir into the sauce. Take the sauce off the heat, stir in the fromage frais and scatter over the coriander.

Serve hot with rice of your choice.

Free on Extra Easy and Original

serves 4

each serving is:

Free on Extra Easy

Free on Original

8 Syns on Green

ready in 45 minutes, plus marinating

---

juice of 1 lime

150g fat free natural yogurt

5 tbsp tikka curry powder

salt and freshly ground black pepper

4 skinless and boneless chicken breasts, cut into bite-sized pieces

low calorie cooking spray

1 onion, grated

4 garlic cloves, crushed

2cm piece of root ginger, peeled and grated

1 red chilli, deseeded and chopped

1 tsp ground cinnamon

1 tsp ground cumin

6 tbsp tomato purée

5 tbsp fat free natural fromage frais

small handful of roughly chopped fresh coriander, to garnish

king prawn
dopiaza //

serves 4

each serving is:

Free on Extra Easy

Free on Original

5 Syns on Green

ready in 40 minutes

---

low calorie cooking spray

2 tbsp medium curry powder

1 tbsp garam masala

2 tsp ground cinnamon

2 tsp ground cumin

2 large onions,
finely chopped

4 garlic cloves, crushed

200ml boiling fish stock

400g can chopped tomatoes

salt and freshly ground
black pepper

500g peeled raw king or tiger
prawns, tails on if you like

small handful of finely
chopped fresh coriander,
to garnish

lime or lemon wedges,
to serve

Dopiaza means 'two onions' so no prizes for guessing the most important ingredient in this memorable curry! Our fakeaway has a deeply smoky flavour thanks to the garam masala and includes plenty of plump and juicy king prawns that the whole family will love.

Spray a large non-stick frying pan with low calorie cooking spray and place over a low heat. Add the spices and cook for about 30 seconds, then add the onions and cook for 3-4 minutes.

Add the garlic, stock and tomatoes and season well. Turn the heat to high and bring to the boil, then reduce the heat to medium-low and cook for 20 minutes, stirring occasionally.

Add the prawns and cook for a further 5-6 minutes, until the prawns turn pink and are cooked through.

Garnish with coriander and serve hot with boiled basmati rice and lime or lemon wedges.

vegetable biryani //

serves 4

each serving is:

Free on Extra Easy

Free on Green

21 Syns on Original

ready in 40 minutes, plus standing

Rice is the star of the show in a biryani and ours is packed with fragrant spices and plenty of tasty vegetables. Feel free to swap in other veg – diced potatoes and small florets of cauliflower and broccoli would all work well.

low calorie cooking spray

3 onions, finely chopped

1cm piece of root ginger, peeled and finely grated

5 garlic cloves, crushed

1 tbsp cumin seeds

2 red chillies, deseeded and finely sliced

100g dried yellow split lentils

200g frozen peas

2 carrots, peeled and roughly chopped

200g green beans, trimmed and chopped

3 tomatoes, chopped

6 cloves

6 cardamom pods, crushed

1 cinnamon stick

1 tsp turmeric

350g dried long-grain rice

salt, to taste

fat free yogurt, sprinkled with paprika or chilli powder, to serve

Spray a large non-stick saucepan with low calorie cooking spray and place over a medium heat. Fry the onions for 5 minutes or until softened then add the ginger, garlic, cumin seeds and most of the chillies and stir-fry for a further 1-2 minutes, stirring frequently.

Add all the remaining ingredients to the saucepan along with 550ml of boiling water and cook for 15-20 minutes. Remove from the heat and leave to stand, still covered, for another 15-20 minutes.

Garnish with the remaining sliced chillies and serve hot with a side dish of fat free natural yogurt sprinkled with paprika or chilli powder.

saag aloo

serves 4

each serving is:

Free on Extra Easy

Free on Green

9½ Syns on Original

❄ Ⓥ

ready in 50 minutes

This is often a side dish on the takeaway menu – our version brings this delicately spiced and very filling meat-free classic into the spotlight!

1kg potatoes, peeled and cut into 2cm cubes

low calorie cooking spray

1 red onion, thinly sliced

2 garlic cloves, crushed

1cm piece of root ginger, peeled and grated

2 tsp cumin seeds

2 tsp black mustard seeds

2 red peppers, deseeded and cut into small pieces

1 tsp ground cumin

1 tsp ground coriander

½ tsp turmeric

½ tsp garam masala

½ tsp chilli powder

salt and freshly ground black pepper

200ml boiling vegetable stock

large bag baby leaf spinach, roughly chopped

small handful of finely chopped fresh coriander, to garnish (optional)

1 red chilli, deseeded and finely sliced, to garnish (optional)

Cook the potatoes in a large saucepan of lightly salted boiling water for 10 minutes or until just tender. Drain thoroughly and set aside.

Spray a non-stick wok or frying pan with low calorie cooking spray and place over a medium-high heat. Add the red onion, garlic, ginger, cumin seeds and mustard seeds and stir-fry for 1-2 minutes. Add the potatoes and peppers and stir-fry for 6-8 minutes or until lightly browned.

Turn the heat to low and add the ground cumin, ground coriander, turmeric, garam masala and chilli powder. Season well and cook for a further 1-2 minutes.

Stir in the stock and bring the mixture to a boil. Turn the heat to medium, cover and cook for 5-6 minutes. Remove from the heat, stir in the spinach and let it wilt into the potato mixture. Season well and scatter over the coriander and chilli, if using.

pilau rice

Our pilau rice is infused with the appealing aromas of cardamom, cloves and cinnamon – it's the perfect accompaniment for your favourite curry.

serves 4

each serving is:

Free on Extra Easy

Free on Green

15½ Syns on Original

ready in 30 minutes, plus soaking and standing

350g dried basmati rice

low calorie cooking spray

1 onion, roughly chopped

6 cardamom pods

8 cloves

6 peppercorns

1 cinnamon stick

1 tsp cumin seeds

a small pinch of saffron threads (or ½ tsp turmeric)

2 bay leaves

500ml boiling vegetable stock or water

salt

Wash the rice in several changes of cold water, then leave to soak in cold water for about 30 minutes.

Spray a non-stick saucepan with low calorie cooking spray and place over a medium heat. Add the onion and cook for about 5 minutes or until softened. Add the spices and bay leaves and cook for a further 2 minutes.

Drain the rice, add to the pan and stir until the grains are coated in the spice mixture. Stir in the stock or water, season with salt and bring to the boil.

Cover with a tight-fitting lid, turn the heat to low and cook for 10 minutes before turning off the heat. Don't remove the lid, just leave the rice in the hot pan for about 10 minutes.

Fluff up the grains and serve hot with your favourite curry.

eastern eats

Satisfy your appetite in style with our Chinese and Thai fakeaways, all packed with filling Free Foods and fabulous far eastern flavours.

heat guide
/ mild
// medium
/// hot

szechuan
beef

serves 4

each serving is:

½ **Syn** on Extra Easy

½ **Syn** on Original

8½ **Syns** on Green

❄

ready in 25 minutes,
plus marinating

---

2 tbsp soy sauce

2 tsp rice vinegar or
white wine vinegar

salt and freshly ground
black pepper

1 level tsp cornflour

2cm piece of root ginger,
peeled and sliced

500g lean beef steak,
visible fat removed, cut into
bite-sized pieces

low calorie cooking spray

2 garlic cloves, crushed

2 red chillies, deseeded
and thinly sliced, plus
extra to garnish

¼ tsp Szechuan
peppercorns, crushed

good pinch of Chinese
five-spice powder

1 red pepper, deseeded
and cut into chunks

1 yellow pepper, deseeded
and cut into chunks

1 spring onion, finely
chopped, to garnish

The food of Szechuan is known for its heat and this fiery dish won't disappoint if you like your Chinese takeaway to pack a punch.

Put the soy sauce, vinegar, ½ teaspoon of salt, cornflour and ginger in a bowl with 1 tablespoon of water and mix together. Add the steak and stir to coat well. Cover and leave to marinate in a cool place for 30 minutes.

Spray a non-stick wok or deep frying pan with low calorie cooking spray and place over a medium-high heat. Add the garlic, chilli, Szechuan peppercorns and five-spice powder and cook for 1 minute. Add the marinated beef (reserving the marinade) and stir-fry for 2-3 minutes. Remove and keep warm.

Add the peppers to the wok and stir-fry for 2 minutes, then return the steak and reserved marinade to the wok. Stir-fry briskly over a medium heat for 1 minute.

Season with plenty of black pepper, scatter over the spring onion and extra chilli and serve hot with rice of your choice.

If you want to tone down the heat, reduce the amount of chilli. If you want more heat, keep the seeds in the chillies when you slice them!

pork in
black bean sauce

serves 4

each serving is:

1 Syn on Extra Easy

1 Syn on Original

8½ Syns on Green

ready in 25 minutes,
plus marinating

500g lean pork fillet,
visible fat removed,
cut into thin strips

2 tbsp soy sauce

1 tbsp sherry

1 level tsp cornflour

1cm piece of root ginger,
peeled and grated

low calorie cooking spray

1 garlic clove, crushed

half a bunch of spring
onions, sliced diagonally

1 green pepper, deseeded
and thinly sliced

1 red pepper, deseeded
and thinly sliced

2 level tbsp black
bean sauce

4 tbsp boiling chicken stock

Black bean sauce is made from fermented soya beans and it brings a delicious saltiness to Chinese dishes. You'll find it at most supermarkets.

Put the pork in a bowl with the soy sauce, sherry, cornflour and ginger. Mix together, then cover and leave in a cool place to marinate for 30 minutes.

Spray a non-stick wok or deep frying pan with low calorie cooking spray and place over a medium-high heat. Add the pork and stir-fry for 5 minutes or until cooked and golden. Remove from the wok and drain on kitchen paper.

Add the garlic, spring onions and peppers to the wok and stir well. Stir-fry for 1 minute over a high heat, then add the black bean sauce and chicken stock. Stir well and return the pork to the wok.

Cover the wok, turn the heat down to medium and cook for 5 minutes, until the liquid has reduced and the pork and vegetables are coated with the sauce. Serve hot with noodles or rice of your choice.

pork
pad thai *

Tasty pork, crunchy veg and the distinctive flavours of garlic, ginger and chilli make this simple Thai noodle dish one that you'll want to make over and over again – and it's Syn-free on Extra Easy!

serves 4

each serving is:

Free on Extra Easy

8 Syns on Green

11½ Syns on Original

ready in 30 minutes

Spray a large non-stick wok or frying pan with low calorie cooking spray and place over a medium-high heat. Add the pork and fry for 3-4 minutes until browned. Add the garlic, ginger, spring onions, stock, soy sauce and Thai fish sauce, turn the heat to low and cook for 5 minutes.

Meanwhile, cook the noodles according to the packet instructions, then drain and set aside.

Add the carrots, pak choi and bean sprouts to the wok and turn the heat to high. Stir-fry for 5 minutes or until the vegetables are just tender.

Add the noodles to the wok, drizzle over the egg and toss to mix well. Cook for 1-2 minutes until the egg is just cooked through then remove from the heat.

Scatter over the chilli and coriander and serve hot with lime halves to squeeze over.

low calorie cooking spray

500g extra-lean pork mince

2 garlic cloves, crushed

1cm piece of root ginger, peeled and finely chopped

bunch of spring onions, sliced diagonally

5 tbsp boiling vegetable stock

2 tbsp dark soy sauce

1 tsp Thai fish sauce (nam pla)

250g dried flat rice noodles

2 carrots, peeled and chopped into matchsticks

2 pak choi, roughly chopped

250g fresh bean sprouts, rinsed

1 egg, lightly beaten

1 red chilli, deseeded and finely chopped

small handful of finely chopped fresh coriander, to serve

lime halves, to serve

sweet and sour chicken

serves 4

each serving is:

3 Syns on Extra Easy

3 Syns on Original

13½ Syns on Green

❄

ready in 30 minutes

This classic Chinese takeaway dish is all about the contrast of sweet and sour – and in our version it's the sweetness of the pineapple and the sour hit of the vinegar and soy sauce that will have you wanting more.

low calorie cooking spray

8 skinless and boneless chicken thighs, cut into bite-sized pieces

1 large onion, roughly chopped

1 green pepper, deseeded and roughly chopped

3 large carrots, peeled and cut into chunks

435g can pineapple chunks in natural juice, drained, reserving 2 tbsp juice

1 garlic clove, crushed

1 level tbsp cornflour

1 tbsp tomato purée

1 tbsp red wine vinegar

2 tbsp soy sauce

finely sliced spring onions, to garnish

Place a non-stick wok or deep frying pan over a high heat and spray with low calorie cooking spray. Add the chicken and cook for 3 minutes, stirring continuously. Transfer the chicken to a plate with a slotted spoon.

Add the onion, pepper and carrots to the wok and cook for 4 minutes, stirring occasionally. Return the chicken to the wok and cook for a further 3-4 minutes until the chicken is cooked through.

Meanwhile, make the sauce by mixing the reserved pineapple juice with the garlic, cornflour, tomato purée, red wine vinegar, soy sauce and 100ml of water.

Stir the sauce into the chicken and vegetables, add the pineapple and cook over a low heat for 2 minutes or until thickened. Scatter over the spring onions and serve hot with noodles or rice.

thai green chicken curry

The UK's favourite Thai takeaway has never been so satisfying or so low in Syns, with generous chunks of chicken thigh and plenty of filling vegetables soaking up the flavours of a warming spicy broth.

Spray a large non-stick wok or frying pan with low calorie cooking spray and place over a medium-high heat. Add the curry paste and chicken and stir-fry for 2-3 minutes. Add the stock and coconut milk and bring to the boil. Reduce the heat, cover and simmer for 10 minutes or until the chicken is cooked through.

Add the vegetables to the wok, bring back to a simmer and cook for 6-8 minutes or until just tender. Remove from the heat, stir in the soy sauce and season to taste.

Ladle the curry into bowls and scatter over the coriander. This is delicious served with Thai fragrant or jasmine rice.

serves 4

each serving is:

1½ **Syns** on Extra Easy

2½ **Syns** on Original

14½ **Syns** on Green

❄

ready in 30 minutes

---

low calorie cooking spray

2 level tbsp Thai green curry paste

8 skinless and boneless chicken thighs, cut into large pieces

600ml boiling chicken stock

100ml light coconut milk

400g frozen mixed vegetables

2 tbsp light soy sauce

salt and freshly ground black pepper

small handful of finely chopped fresh coriander, to garnish

chicken chow mein /

serves 4

each serving is:

½ **Syn** on Extra Easy

8½ **Syns** on Green

16½ **Syns** on Original

ready in 35 minutes,
plus marinating

---

4 tbsp light soy sauce

2 tsp Chinese rice vinegar
or white wine vinegar

4 garlic cloves, crushed

2cm piece of root ginger,
peeled and grated

1 tsp Chinese
five-spice powder

4 skinless and boneless
chicken breasts, cut into
bite-sized pieces

350g dried egg noodles

low calorie cooking spray

1 carrot, peeled,
halved and sliced

200g mangetout, halved
lengthways

225g can water chestnuts,
drained

225g can bamboo shoots,
drained

1 red pepper, deseeded
and sliced

100g baby sweetcorn,
halved lengthways

bunch of spring onions,
sliced diagonally

60g fresh bean sprouts,
rinsed

1 level tbsp oyster sauce

2 tbsp dark soy sauce

½ tsp toasted sesame oil

We've packed this classic noodle stir-fry with oodles of flavour and an abundance of healthy vegetables – saving you 16 Syns on Extra Easy.

Mix the light soy sauce, vinegar, garlic, ginger and five-spice powder in a bowl. Add the chicken, toss to coat evenly and leave to marinate in a cool place for 20 minutes.

Meanwhile, cook the noodles according to the packet instructions then drain and set aside.

Spray a non-stick wok or large frying pan with low calorie cooking spray and place over a high heat. Add the chicken mixture and stir-fry for 5 minutes or until lightly browned.

Add the carrot, mangetout, water chestnuts, bamboo shoots, red pepper, sweetcorn and spring onions and stir-fry for 5 minutes.

Add the noodles, bean sprouts, oyster sauce, dark soy sauce and sesame oil and toss everything together. Cook for a further 4 minutes and serve hot.

thai fish cakes //

serves 4

each serving is:

Free on Extra Easy

Free on Original

11 Syns on Green

❄ (uncooked fish cakes only)

ready in about 30 minutes, plus chilling

600g peeled raw king or tiger prawns, roughly chopped

500g skinless and boneless cod fillet, roughly chopped

2 red chillies, deseeded and finely chopped, plus extra to garnish

bunch of spring onions, roughly chopped

2 lemon grass stalks, outer leaves removed, roughly chopped

finely grated zest of 4 unwaxed limes, plus wedges to serve

1 tsp Thai fish sauce (nam pla)

large handful of finely chopped fresh coriander

salt and freshly ground black pepper

low calorie cooking spray

These sensational fish cakes are so easy to make and they're full of amazing flavours. Serve with noodles to make a meal or have them on their own as a mouth-watering starter.

Put the prawns, cod, chillies, spring onions, lemon grass, lime zest, Thai fish sauce and coriander in a food processor and whizz until fairly smooth. Season, mix well and transfer to a bowl. Cover and chill for 4 hours or overnight if you have time.

When you're ready to cook, preheat your oven to 180°C/Fan 160°C/Gas 4 and line a baking tray with baking parchment.

Divide the fish mixture into 20 portions, then shape into cakes and arrange on the prepared tray. Spray with low calorie cooking spray and bake for 15-20 minutes or until cooked through, turning halfway.

Divide the fish cakes between plates, scatter over the extra chilli and serve hot with noodles and lime wedges to squeeze over.

These fish cakes are fantastic served with sweet chilli sauce (1½ Syns per tablespoon).

special prawn fried rice

serves 4

each serving is:

½ **Syn** on Extra Easy

4½ **Syns** on Green

17 **Syns** on Original

ready in 30 minutes

Our fakeaway version of the takeaway classic is a meal in itself, with every mouthful packed full of juicy prawns and mushrooms.

350g dried long-grain or Thai fragrant/jasmine rice

low calorie cooking spray

2 eggs

1 onion, finely chopped

150g mushrooms, finely sliced

400g peeled raw king or tiger prawns

125g frozen peas, thawed

2 tbsp soy sauce

2 level tbsp oyster sauce

Cook the rice according to the packet instructions, then drain and cool under cold running water.

Meanwhile, spray a large non-stick wok or deep frying pan with a little low calorie cooking spray and place over a medium-high heat. Whisk the eggs in a small jug with 1 tablespoon of water, pour into the wok and cook for 2 minutes. Turn the omelette, cook for 1 more minute, then remove from the pan and set aside to cool.

Add a little more low calorie cooking spray to the wok, turn the heat down to medium and cook the onion, mushrooms and prawns for 5-6 minutes, until the prawns are pink and nearly cooked through. Add the cooled rice and cook for a further 4 minutes, then add the peas and cook for 2 minutes.

Slice the omelette into thin strips and add to the rice with the soy sauce and oyster sauce. Fold everything together for a minute to heat through and serve hot.

speedy vegetable noodles with tofu

serves 4

each serving is:

½ **Syn** on Extra Easy

½ **Syn** on Green

16 **Syns** on Original

ⓥ

ready in 25 minutes

350g dried egg noodles

3 tbsp light soy sauce

4 garlic cloves, crushed

2cm piece of root ginger, peeled and finely grated

1 tsp Chinese five-spice powder

low calorie cooking spray

200g mangetout, trimmed and halved

100g shiitake mushrooms, sliced

1 red pepper, halved, deseeded and thinly sliced

bunch of spring onions, sliced diagonally

1 pak choi, roughly chopped

1 level tbsp sweet chilli sauce

2 tbsp dark soy sauce

300g firm tofu (plain or naturally smoked), cut into large cubes

Tofu is a delicious alternative to meat – and it's just one of the highlights in this sizzling medley of flavours.

Cook the noodles according to the packet instructions then drain and set aside.

In a bowl, mix together the light soy sauce, garlic, ginger and Chinese five-spice powder and set aside.

Spray a large non-stick wok or frying pan with low calorie cooking spray and place over a high heat. Add all the vegetables apart from the pak choi and stir-fry for 5 minutes or until just tender. Add the garlic and ginger mixture and stir-fry for 2-3 minutes.

Add the noodles, pak choi, sweet chilli sauce, dark soy sauce and tofu pieces and toss together for 3-4 minutes. Serve hot in warmed bowls.

thai yellow vegetable curry

serves 4

each serving is:

1 Syn on Extra Easy

1 Syn on Green

1 Syn on Original

ready in 30 minutes

This home-made curry paste is a taste sensation and it really gives vegetables the VIP treatment.

First put all the curry paste ingredients in a food processor and blend until smooth. Transfer to a saucepan over a medium heat and gently bring to the boil.

Add the sweetcorn, aubergine, courgettes and red pepper to the curry paste and bring back to the boil. Reduce the heat to low and simmer for 10-12 minutes, stirring frequently until the vegetables are cooked.

Garnish with the coriander sprigs and sliced chilli and serve hot, with boiled Thai fragrant or jasmine rice.

You can leave out the coconut milk to make this curry Free on all choices. Add an extra 100ml of stock instead.

200g baby sweetcorn

1 aubergine, cubed

2 courgettes, cubed

1 red pepper, deseeded and cut into bite-sized pieces

fresh coriander sprigs, to garnish

1 red chilli, deseeded and sliced, to garnish

for the yellow curry paste

1-2 green chillies, deseeded and roughly chopped

2 shallots, roughly chopped

2cm piece of root ginger, peeled and grated

4 garlic cloves, crushed

1 tsp ground coriander

1 tsp ground cumin

¼ tsp ground cinnamon

3 tbsp dark soy sauce

1 tsp turmeric

¼ tsp sweetener

4 kaffir lime leaves, stems discarded

100ml light coconut milk

200ml boiling vegetable stock

1 lemon grass stalk, outer leaves removed, roughly chopped

egg fried rice

A Chinese meal isn't complete without a bowl of the classic rice dish and it's so easy to make at home.

350g dried long-grain or Thai fragrant/jasmine rice

2 eggs

low calorie cooking spray

150g frozen peas, thawed

bunch of spring onions, roughly chopped

2 tbsp soy sauce

ground white pepper

Cook the rice according to the packet instructions then cool under cold running water and set aside.

Meanwhile, beat the eggs with 2 tablespoons of water.

Spray a non-stick wok or large frying pan with low calorie cooking spray. When it's almost smoking, add the cooked rice and stir-fry for about 3-4 minutes until completely heated through.

Add the peas and spring onions to the wok and stir-fry for about 3 minutes, making sure the rice doesn't stick. Stir the soy sauce and pepper into the rice and push it to one side of the wok.

Pour the beaten egg mixture into the other side of the wok and leave for about 10 seconds until it begins to set. Briskly swirl through the egg with a chopstick to break it up then toss it through the rice. Stir-fry for a further minute and serve hot with your favourite Chinese fakeaway.

Sweet chilli sauce (1½ Syns per tablespoon) is great with egg fried rice.

index

Published in 2014 by
Slimming World
Clover Nook Road
Somercotes
Alfreton
Derbyshire
DE55 4SW
UK
www.slimmingworld.com

Created and designed by
Slimming World's publications team.
Publications manager: Allison Brentnall
Editor: Oliver Maxey
Designer: Kathryn Briggs

Recipes and food styling: Sunil Vijayakar
Photographs: Gareth Morgans
Styling: Morag Farquhar

Front cover photograph:
Special prawn fried rice, page 110

Back cover photographs, from left:
SW spiced chicken, page 62
Battered fish and chips, pages 30 and 41
Double bacon burgers, page 12
Griddled Mediterranean vegetable pizza, page 50

did you know?

10p from the sale of this book goes to our charitable foundation SMILES (Slimmers Making it a Little Easier for Someone), whose charity partners have included the NSPCC, Barnardo's, Cancer Research UK and the Marie Keating Foundation. Last year we donated £100,000 from book sales.